DL 129
GRADES 4-6

Understanding Advertising

HISTORY

PERSUASION TECHNIQUES

MASS MEDIA

TARGET AUDIENCES

AD CREATION

Written by **Katherine Howe** and **Judith Edelstein**
Illustrated by **Mary Lou Johnson**

Edited by Dianne Draze and Sonsie Conroy

ISBN 1-883055-37-7

Contents

Information for the Instructor

We live in a sea of advertising. It is everywhere we look. It dominates television and radio programming and pops up on your computer screen each time you use the Internet. It's hard to escape the all-pervasive influence of advertising. Since advertisements affect how people spend their time and money, they can, hopefully become more discriminating consumers if they are aware of the techniques that advertisers use to get them to buy their products and services.

The field of advertising uses special forms of creative expression and psychology in order to persuade. The intent of this book is to introduce students to advertising and how it affects their lives and buying decisions. The more students know about advertising, the more they will be able to judge whether information that is presented to them in advertisements is valid and whether they are buying the products or services because these things are something they need or whether they are being drawn into the purchase because of psychological motivators. It gives them one more tool in being independent, well-informed consumers. The other objective of this book is to provide students with the tools for creating advertisements and to present an outlet for creative thinking. As they create their own advertisements, they will be using both critical and creative thinking.

As a result of completing the activities in this study unit students will:

- Become familiar with terminology used in the field of advertising
- Become familiar with language that advertisers use to create their ads
- Determine how advertising affects their personal purchasing decisions
- Investigate several factors that motivate consumer purchases
- Be able to differentiate between the different media and decide why an advertiser would choose one medium over another
- Create a marketing plan for a product
- Compare the effectiveness of commercials
- Use effective advertising techniques to create their own advertisements

This book provides an easy-to-use format that incorporates several different ways to present information. **Lesson plans** provide step-by-step instructions for group lessons. Each lesson also has a list of suggested **extensions** for projects that will give students opportunities to present information about advertising in creative ways. **Worksheets** are reproducible pages that present information about different aspects of advertising and either provide ways to apply knowledge or guidelines for projects. As a whole, this unit is a complete guide for introducing students to all the most important concepts in advertising.

Group Lessons

Lesson 1 - What is Advertising?

Objective
Students will be able to define and provide examples of advertising and relate advertising to persuasion.

Materials
newspapers, magazines, worksheets:
"What is Advertising?" page 16
"The Advertising Advantage," page 17
"Different Points of View," page 18

Procedure

1. Provide students with various situations in which they are to persuade another student to do something. Examples might include:
   - a boy asking a girl for a date
   - someone wanting to borrow a favorite game
   - a child asking a parent to stay out late
   - a girl convincing a friend to go bowling instead of skating
   - someone asking for a loan
   Act out several of the situations.

2. Discuss the tactics that each person used. Have students provide examples of tactics they use to persuade someone to do something.

3. Define advertising as an attempt to get people to buy a product, use a service, or accept an idea.

4. As a group, make a list of all the places one would find advertising.

5. Go through the worksheet entitled "What is Advertising?" and discuss the components of advertising.

6. Divide students into small groups and ask each group to provide an example of advertising that is selling a product, selling a service and selling an idea. They should identify the advertisement, what it is trying to persuade people to do and where the advertisement is found (television, radio, magazine, etc.). Go around and check their choices and then have each group share their selections with the whole class.

Extensions

Examples - Ask students to look through newspapers and magazines and find an examples of advertisements that:
   - are informative
   - introduce a new product
   - make an offer (like a reduced price)
   - announce a sale or special event
Cut out the examples, mount and label them.

Charting Advertising - Consult a current almanac. Make a chart that shows one of the following:
   - advertising expenditures in our country over the last 100 years (show 25-year increments)
   - money spent on advertising by the top ten advertisers in our country
   - percentage of advertising dollars spent in each medium (newspapers, magazines, television, radio, direct mail, outdoor, other)

Advertising Advantage - Have students do the worksheet entitled "The Advertising Advantage," page 17. Discuss their thoughts.

Different Points of View - Have students do the worksheet entitled "Different Points of View," page 18. After they have completed the worksheet, divide students into groups, and assign a different individual to represent each point of view. Have them discuss advertising, each person presenting his or her assigned point of view.

Lesson 2 - History of Advertising

Objective
Students will be able to identify which forms of advertising have been used in the past and which would be appropriate for various businesses.

Materials
worksheet entitled "History of Adverting," pages 19 and 20

Procedure

1. Ask students how they think people advertised their products and services before there were radio, televison and the Internet.

2. Go through the "History of Advertising" worksheet. Discuss the following concepts:

   - When everyone produced only enough for their own existence, there was no need to advertise. Once people began producing more products than they and their families could consume, they needed to advertise so other people would know what they had for sale.
   - Early advertising was just to inform people of what was available. There was no attempt to persuade people.
   - Most early advertising did not involve writing because most people could not read.
   - The invention of the moveable type printing press opened up new avenues for advertising.
   - The Industrial Revolution meant that there was an abundance of products available and people had to look for new markets for these products. This meant that advertising was greatly expanded beyond the local region of the producer.

3. Ask students to get into groups of two. Each group should choose a business that might have been available during the 1600s. They should decide what they would like to tell their neighbors about their products or services. After they have prepared what a barker would say about their business, one or both of them should perform the advertisement as a barker would. They can embellish their performance with sandwich boards, signs, and jingles.

Extensions
Time Line - Have students make an illustrated time line of advertising.

Store Signs - Merchant's store signs used to be pictures of what service they offered or products they sold. Assign students different types of stores or services and have them create signs for these businesses.

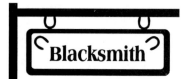 

Lesson 3 - Appealing to Human Needs

Objective
Students will be able to identify advertisements that appeal to various human needs.

Materials
worksheets entitled:
"Meeting Human Needs," page 21
"What's the Appeal?," page 22
"What Appeals to You?," page 23

Procedure

1. Pose the question, "What do you really need to survive?" Discuss the basic human needs (food, water, shelter, self-preservation).

2. Tell students that while humans' basic needs are food, water, shelter and self-preservation, to be happy, fulfilled individuals, we have other needs. As a group, make a list of things that students feel they need.

3. On the board write the categories:

health	security
prosperity	approval
self-fulfillment	attraction
comfort	pleasure

   Go through the list of things that students provided and identify a need category for each one. For instance, "friends" would be "approval" and "heating and cooling" would be "comfort."

4. Explain that successful advertising will appeal to one of these human needs. If the advertiser does not present the product as fulfilling a need, it will be harder to convince people to buy it.

5. Go through the worksheet entitled "Meeting Human Needs."

Extensions
Identifying Appeals - Have students complete the worksheets entitled "What is the Appeal?" to identify the appeal in different advertising statements.
Answers: 1. health 2. prosperity 3. prosperity
4. approval 5. comfort 6. health 7. prosperity
8. security 9. security 10. approval
11. attraction 12. health/comfort 13. health
14. pleasure 15. approval

Give Examples - Have students find statements in advertisements or make up their own statements that demonstrate an appeal to each of the human needs.

Personal Introspection - Have students examine their own motivators by completing the worksheet entitled "What Appeals to You?"

Lesson 4 - Other Persuasion Techniques

Objective
Students will be able to identify other persuasive techniques used in advertising.

Materials
worksheet entitled "Hidden Persuaders," page 24

Procedure
1. Go through the information on the worksheet entitled "Hidden Persuaders." Discuss the techniques and ask students to provide examples from advertisements that they have seen on television or heard on the radio.

2. Give students the following statements and ask them to identify the techniques that are being used.
   - The Smart Choice (image)
   - Don't Wait! Join all your friends at the back-to-school picnic. (bandwagon)
   - Nine out of ten of the best chefs use Cutright cutlery (testimonial)

- Be a truly gourmet cook. Use Cutright cutlery. (image)
- Don't use knives that will get dull after only a few uses. Use Cutright cutlery. (name calling)
- Even Aunt Margaret thinks her apple pies are better when she uses Cutright cutlery. (plain folks)
- Head-Ease will cure most headaches in most people. (weasel)
- Most doctors prescribed Head-Ease for minor headaches. (testimonial/weasel)
- Don't settle for mediocre service at the other tire stores. Stop by Zac's Tires for service you can depend on. (name calling)
- You can have as nice a yard as your neighbors with Gro-More fertilizer. (image)
- You don't need a lot of money to drive a car that says "I'm somebody." (image)

Extension
Display - Collect advertisements that are examples of these persuasive techniques. Make a display of these advertisements and tell which technique is used in each example.

Lesson 5 - Mass Media

Objective
Students will be able to identify various forms of mass media, explain the advantages of advertising in each one and compare the different types of media.

Materials
worksheets entitled:
"Get the Message Out," page 25
"The Cost of Advertising," page 26
"Selling Your Product," page 27
"Ad Time," page 28

Procedure
1. Give students one minute to list all the things they would like to buy if they had the money to buy anything they wanted.

2. Then have students tell where they heard about each product. Make a list of sources of information.

3. Discuss what mass media is and how it influences people's buying decisions. Point out the mutual benefit that advertising offers to both advertisers and media owners. Advertising lets business owners tell potential customers about their products and services, and the owners of media receive money by running the ads.

4. Go through the worksheet "Getting the Message Out." Give students the following products and services. Ask them which medium would work best for each product or service.
   • beauty salon
   • a movie showing at the local theater
   • a new kind of vitamins
   • bridal dresses
   • a local radio station
   • a motel and restaurant
   • an organization that tries to get people to wear seat belts
   • an organization that is raising money to buy land for a local park
   • in-line skates
   • dentist

Extension
Advertisements - Have each student choose a product and create an advertisement for that product in two different media; for instance, radio and a billboard. Have them tell which would be the most effective and why.

Media Comparison - Using the worksheets on pages 26 - 27 have students compare various aspects of media advertising.

Guest Speakers - Bring in guest speakers from radio, television, newspapers, marketing firms or advertising agencies to discuss how advertising relates to their particular medium.

Lesson 6 - Radio

Objective
Students will be able to use techniques of radio advertising to make their own advertisements.

Materials
worksheets entitled "Radio Advertising," page 29 and "Radio Script," page 30.

Procedure
1. Ask students to think about these comparisons and share their thoughts:
   • In what ways is a ball park like a subway?
   • How can tenderness be heard?

2. Discuss the importance of sound in our lives and, specifically, in advertising. Ask, "What form of advertising relies solely on sound?"

3. Discuss which radio advertisements are the most convincing and why. Discuss techniques used in these advertisements, like the use of repetition, rhyme, verse, jingles, music, and sound effects.

4. Go through the worksheet entitled "Radio Advertising."

5. Give students the sample radio script on page 30. Divide the class into small groups and have them develop their own scripts for a radio advertisement using this format.

Lesson 7 - Television

Objective
Students will be able to identify techniques used in television advertising and create their own advertisements.

Materials
prerecorded video of selected television advertisements, the following worksheets:
"More Ways to Sell," page 31
"Matching Advertising and Audiences," page 32
"Television Advertising Survey," page 33
"Your Own Television Commercial," page 34

Procedure
1. Record several television commercials and view them in class. Discuss each commercial. What makes students want to purchase each product? Go through the worksheet entitled "More Ways to Sell."

2. Discuss what techniques television advertisers use. Refer back to the list of persuasive techniques from page 24. Have students give examples of television advertisements that use these techniques.

3. Discuss how different products are advertised on various programs depending on what kind of viewer will likely be viewing that show. Ask students what kind of products would be advertised on the following shows:
   - children's cartoon
   - home and gardening
   - family situation comedy
   - national football
   - local news program

4. Have students do the worksheet entitled "Matching Advertising and Audiences."

Extensions

TV Log - Use the worksheet on page 33 to complete a log of techniques used in television advertisements.

Song - Have students compose original jingles or songs to advertise products.

Storyboard - Explain the use of story boards to show the sequence of events that will be depicted on television or in movies. Using page 34, have students create their own advertisements and make storyboards to illustrate the ads.

Lesson 8 - Print Advertising

Objective
Students will be able to identify techniques that make effective print advertisements and create their own advertisements.

Materials
magazines, newspapers, the following worksheets:
"Newspaper Advertising," page 35
"Language of Advertising," page 36
"Attention Getters," page 37
"Analyzing Print Ads," page 38

Procedure

1. Identify print ads as any advertisement that appears in printed mass media (newspapers, magazines, catalogs, and flyers). Divide the class into small groups and give each group a couple of newspapers or magazines. Ask them to choose several advertisements and identify the hidden persuaders in each ad.

2. Then ask them to analyze the use of color, headlines, positioning of the product, descriptive words, and any other elements that make the advertisements more appealing.

3. Have each group choose one ad that they think is particularly effective or attention-getting and explain to the rest of the class what they find appealing about this ad.

4. Compare advertisements found in newspapers to those in magazines. Ask students to explain how they are the same and different.

5. Use the worksheet entitled "Newspaper Advertising" to have students tabulate what kind of businesses advertise in your local newspaper.

6. Use the worksheets entitled "The Language of Advertising" to acquaint students with words that are frequently used in print advertisements. Ask them to check advertisements in the newspaper to find ads that use these words. Then have them create advertisements that use these words.

7. Use the worksheet entitled "Attention Getters" to introduce the common elements of print ads. Follow up with the worksheet entitled "Analyzing Print Ads" to have students identify these elements in a real advertisement.

Extensions

Ad Creation - Have students apply their understanding of the elements of print advertising by choosing a product and designing a print ad for the product.

Improvement - Have students demonstrate the importance of aesthetics in print ads by finding a boring, uninteresting advertisement and turning it into an advertisement that is pleasing and attention-getting. Have them mount both advertisements together on a piece of paper.

Self Ad - Have students create advertisements of themselves, stressing their good points and special talents or skills.

Lesson 9 - Living Up to Claims

Objective
Students will be able to state a hypothesis about product performance and then test the products to see if it meets the stated criteria.

Materials
paper products, worksheets:
"Product Evaluation," page 39
"Advertising Watchdogs," page 40

Procedure

1. Explain that products have to be able to measure up to any claims made in advertisements. Producers cannot make claims that are false or deceitful. If they say that their product is strongest, softest, most absorbent, preferred by 9 out of 10 doctors, etc., these claims have to be true. For this reason, producers will usually test their products to make sure all claims can be substantiated.

2. Ask each student to choose a paper product (paper towel, tissues, etc.).

3. Then students should develop hypotheses about their products and test the hypothesis. They might write hypotheses like:
   - Brand A absorbs more water than the other two leading paper towels.
   - Brand B tissue will not irritate your nose after repeated usage.
   - Brand C paper plates will not allow food to leak through.
   - Brand D paper cups will hold water longer than the other two brands.
   - The more you pay for napkins, the more they will absorb.

4. After their tests, students should write up the results of their experiments.

5. Finally, they can create advertisements for any media to communicate the findings of their tests.

Extensions
Other Experiments - Repeat the tests with other products. Some ideas for products and things to test are:
toys - durability or safety
batteries - length of life
electronic games - interest
frozen food - home-made taste
clothes - colorfast, durable, won't shrink
Use the worksheet on page 39 to keep track of results.

Monitoring Agencies - Use the worksheet entitled "Advertising Watch Dogs," to go through some of the agencies that regulate or monitor advertisements to make sure they are truthful.

Evaluation and Recreation - Have students find examples of advertisements (print or television) that they think are offensive, deceptive, or inappropriate. Then have them recreate the advertisements to be more truthful or tasteful.

Analysis - Have students choose several advertisements and analyze what is not said or what information is missing. Then have them write several questions regarding the missing information.

Culminating Activities

Comparison - Using the worksheets entitled "Advertisement Comparison," (page 41-43) have students compare advertisements for two different products. This is an extensive comparison of advertisements for similar products and provides a good review of all the concepts that have been presented in this book.

Creative Thinking - Ask students to explain how advertising is like each of the following:
- a beacon
- the fog
- a checking account
- a filter
- a telephone
- a friendly dog

Survey - Have students choose three different products and then conduct surveys of their families and classmates to see which products other people find most appealing and whether they are persuaded by the advertisement or the package design. Use page 44 to record the results.

Debates - Advertising offers a good venue for debating. Page 45 suggests several topics for debates, but after studying this unit, students may be able to suggest additional issues. Divide students into teams for the debates, with one side arguing the issue as stated and one arguing the opposite stance.

Advertising Campaign - Using page 46, have students create a whole advertising campaign for a business. This will involve selecting the media in which to advertise and then creating the ads.

New Product - Use the worksheet entitled "Wacky Product" on page 47 to have students create a new product and design an advertisement for it. They can choose to do a radio, television or print ad.

Feelings about Advertising - Have students take a survey to find out how people feel about advertising. They should design a survey instrument that will allow them to find out if people think advertising is informative, untruthful, exaggerated, false, misleading, annoying, entertaining, helpful, or creative (or some other reaction). Have them submit their findings and make a chart to visually represent the results.

Personal Assessment - Use the worksheet entitled "Advertising and You" on page 48 to have students assess how advertising affects them and how their new knowledge about advertising techniques will affect future purchasing behavior.

Advertising Vocabulary

Write a definition for each of these terms.

advertising _____
_____

advertising agency _____
_____

advertiser _____
_____

broadcast media _____
_____

commercial _____
_____

consumer _____
_____

direct mail advertising _____
_____

headline _____
_____

market research (market testing, market survey) _____

_____

marketing _____

_____

mass media _____

_____

print advertisement _____

_____

promotional mix _____

_____

publicity _____

_____

sales talk _____

_____

storyboard _____

_____

target audience _____

_____

What Is Advertising?

Marketing is all the business activities that are associated with getting goods from the producer to the customer. Included in marketing is developing the products, distributing the goods and promoting them to the customers.

Advertising is a vital part of the promotion part of marketing. It is a sales message that is designed to persuade people to buy a product or service or adopt a viewpoint. Advertising is an important part of marketing because, while manufacturers can make goods that are appealing, unless people know about the goods and are persuaded to try them, the products will remain unsold.

You find advertising all around you. It can be as obvious as the commercials on your television and the advertisements that fill your mail box or as subtle as a sign in a store window. You are in constant contact with advertising messages; messages that are trying to tell you how to think, what to buy or who to turn to for help. All of this advertising has four common elements. They are:

- **sales message** - The message is designed to convince the customer of the merits of the product or service.
- **mass audience** - The advertising message can reach a large number of people through the mass media (newspapers, magazines, television, etc.).
- **goods, services or ideas** - The advertising message asks people to buy a product, use a service, or believe an idea.
- **advertiser pays** - The advertiser or sponsor, pays for preparing the advertisement and inserting it in the media. This is different from publicity, which is a free message about the product or company.

Special Project

Goods or Services? - List at least ten different businesses in your town. For each one, indicate whether the business provides goods, services or both. Put a ★ by each business you can recall seeing or hearing an advertisement for during the last month.

The Advertising Advantage

Large sums of money are spent every year for advertising. Advertising benefits many different people. Not only do business owners need to let potential customers know about their businesses and products, but the media (newspapers, radio, television, magazines) need to make a profit. This has lead to a natural union of the two forces. Businesses commonly pay for space or time to advertise their products in media that will reach a large number of people who are their potential customers.

Think about advertising from these different points of view.

What are the advantages of advertising for:

the advertiser _____

_____

the consumer _____

_____

the owners of the media_____

_____

Are there disadvantages? If so, what are they? _____

_____

_____

_____

What people or groups might criticize advertising? What might their criticisms be?_____

_____

_____

Different Points of View

How might the following people view advertising? Write a brief statement to express their views or concerns.

manufacturer of the product

director of an advertising agency

Better Business Bureau

manufacturer of a competing product

parents of children

mass media

consumer with limited income

© Dandy Lion Publications - *Understanding Advertising*

History of Advertising

Ancient Times

Advertising is as old as commerce. Historical documents confirm that advertising was used in ancient times. Early advertising, however, was designed to announce what the merchant had for sale and remind people to buy it. It did not attempt to persuade people to buy the product. The persuasion factor did not enter advertising until the advent of printing.

Until the introduction of printing, advertising was limited to shop signs, town criers and "barkers" and wall signs. Merchants hung signs outside of their places of business to identify their trades or what products they sold. They were not able to use any printed announcements because only the very wealthy elite could read. What merchants could not tell with their store signs (how fresh their fish was or how tasty their meat pies were), they hired criers to walk the streets and call out to residents of the village. They also hung signs and posters in public meeting places.

Roman Empire and Dark Ages

During the time when the Roman Empire was at its height, advertising included store signs and criers, but merchants also painted signs on the sides of buildings, forming an early version of billboards. During the Dark Ages, however, shops were often robbed and destroyed, so merchants did not want to draw attention to the fact that they had valuable goods. During this period, town criers were used to tell the town's residents about important news. At the end of the Dark Ages when living conditions improved, town criers took on the roles of advertising criers, walking through the town, noisily telling people about merchants' goods and merchants began using shop signs again.

Printing Brings Changes

Printing originated in China in about 800 A.D., but Gutenberg's invention of a printing press using moveable type in 1456 made education available to more people. Merchants were able to use printed posters, handbills, signs, pamphlets, and newspapers for advertising their wares. It was common to have printed signs tacked up in public places.

The first newspaper was printed in England in 1622, and by the early 1700s advertisements flourished in newspapers. When Europeans colonized the North American continent, they brought with them the now-familiar forms of advertising. Benjamin Franklin was an especially notable writer of clever advertisements for his newspapers.

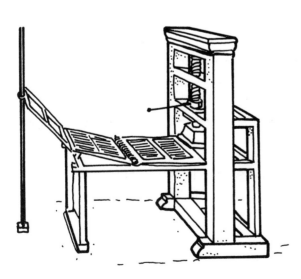

The Industrial Revolution
New Products, New Markets

The advent of the Industrial Revolution made large-circulation newspapers possible and allowed advertisements to reach more people. As businesses began producing more products using the new mechanical inventions, they needed expanded markets in which to sell their products. The increased use of advertising was aided by the spread of education. Because more people could read and write, written advertisements became a good way to reach these potential customers.

The Advent of Electronic Media

The first commercial radio broadcast was in 1920, and by 1948, television was being broadcast into a large number of homes. The introduction of these two media meant that advertising could be brought right into the customers' homes. Since now nearly every home has a radio and a television and these two media offer opportunities for more attention-getting advertisements, they have become powerful means of introducing new products and ideas. The introduction of the Internet in 1992 has given advertisers an additional way to reach their customers and persuade them to buy their products and services. Today advertisers include not only stores and manufacturers selling products but also political candidates, the government, charitable organizations, and groups supporting special causes.

Special Project

The year is 1650. Decide what kind of advertising each of these businesses would use. Choose two occupations and for each one make the appropriate form(s) of advertising this person would use — a shop sign, a poster or notice to be posted in a public place, and/or dialogue for a crier.

a barber	a baker	a pharmacist
an innkeeper	a lawyer	a shoemaker

Meeting Human Needs

If advertisers are going to motivate people to buy their products, services or ideas, they must employ psychology. Advertising does a better job of motivating people to buy a product if the advertising appeals to some human need. People's basic needs are for food, water, clothing, shelter and self-preservation. Once these basic needs are met, people put their energy into satisfying other needs. If the product does not fulfill one of these needs, chances are that only a few people will be convinced to buy it. In creating ads, advertisers should take into consideration the following needs:

Basic human needs:

    food, water, shelter, self-preservation

Other human needs:

- **health** - well-being and physical health; a good night's sleep, not being sick, not being overweight, having energy

- **security** - protection against financial disaster, fire, accidents, or crime

- **prosperity** - wealth and financial security; increased profits, value for money, increased income

- **approval** - being accepted, respected, liked and looked up to

- **self-fulfillment** - being able to take advantage of one's abilities and develop them fully

- **attraction** - becoming more attractive, appealing or charming to members of the opposite sex

- **comfort** - feeling as comfortable as possible; this includes products and services that not only make you comfortable but are easy and convenient to use

- **pleasure** - having fun and good times

Special Project

For each human need, identify a product that could be advertised using this appeal.

What's the Appeal?

Here are statements that you might find in advertisements. For each one, identify which human need the statement is referring to.

1. Twice as many vitamins as real oranges   _____
2. Guaranteed to save you at least 25%   _____
3. For people who only want the very best   _____
4. Be admired by everyone in your school   _____
5. Stay cool during the hottest summer days   _____
6. Only brand X gives you all-day relief from your headaches   _____
7. Get that higher-paying job you deserve   _____
8. Keeps you and your family safe from home robberies   _____
9. The safest car on the road   _____
10. Be the envy of your neighborhood   _____
11. Do men prefer blondes? Try Blondie Dye and find out   _____
12. Lose weight and feel great with our easy-to-use plan   _____
13. Wake up feeling great every morning   _____
14. A movie sure to leave you rolling in the aisles   _____
15. Your children will think you're the best mom on the block   _____

What Appeals to You?

Make a check by the statements that would get your attention and maybe persuade you to purchase the product or service.

____ This is what everyone will be wearing this fall.

____ Nine out of ten doctors recommend this product.

____ This is the tennis shoe all our Olympic runners will be wearing.

____ Get name-brand quality at an economical price.

____ Unlike the other stores, you won't find big crowds or pushy salespeople at our store.

____ Feel safe wherever you go.

____ It's the most fun you've ever had.

____ Everyone will want to come to your party.

____ Have all the money you need.

____ Be the star of your team.

____ Get rid of those uncomfortable shoes and walk easy forever.

____ All you can eat — One low price.

____ Are you sick of being picked on?

____ Double your pleasure, double your fun.

Hidden Persuaders

The more advertisements you hear or see, the more you will become aware of the special techniques that advertisers use to persuade you to buy their products. They use subtle ways of stating their messages and making people feel like they want to buy the products. These are techniques that are used in conjunction with an appeal to a human need. You will find these same techniques used in all media (television, magazines, newspapers, and radio).

The most common persuasive techniques are:

- **Bandwagon** - Join the crowd. Everyone's buying it, wearing it, doing it.

- **Testimonial** - A famous person or an authority on the subject says the product is good.

- **Plain Folks** - People in the advertisement appear to be average, typical people, leading you to believe that the product is for everyone.

- **Name Calling** - Making the product seem better by using unpopular terms about the competition.

- **Image Advertising** - A product is associated with certain people, places, sounds, or activities. Often the implied message is that you will be young and attractive, be well-liked, appear wealthy, have a good time or have a more enjoyable time if you use this product.

- **Weasel** - A message or promise is implied but not definite. It uses words like "usually" or "chances are this might help you."

Special Project

Write one or more statements for each technique that would demonstrate what an advertiser might say in an advertisement that uses this approach.

Getting the Message Out

Mass media is a form of communication that reaches a large number of people. Advertisers are interested in getting their messages out to as many people as possible. For this reason, they choose to broadcast their messages in the various forms of media that will reach a lot of people. Advertising provides the major portion of the profits for many forms of media.

The ways that advertisers can get their message to people include:

newspaper - Advertisements appear in each section of the paper and usually appeal to people who would be most interested in that particular section. Local papers reach only the people living in an area and are usually not kept for a long period of time.

broadcast media - Television and radio offer commercial time during every program. These media offer ways to reach a large number of people.

magazines - Print ads are designed to appeal to the subscribers of the particular magazine. These also reach a large number of people and are a way to target people who have particular interests, tastes, or professions.

outdoor media - Posters, signs or billboards are posted along roadways and in public places.

transit advertising - Ads on public transportation provide a local focus.

direct mail - Advertising is sent through the mail directly to the prospective customers' homes. These can be catalogs, fliers, postcards, or computer disks.

Internet - Banner ads are flashed on the pages of many websites and many websites are devoted exclusively to advertising products.

specialities - These include giveaways like calendars, pens, T-shirts, or cups.

 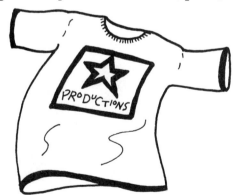 

Special Project

For each medium, identify several products that are well-suited to be advertised in that medium.

The Cost of Advertising

As you might guess, it costs a lot of money to advertise. Besides the costs of preparing the advertisement, the medium (newspaper, radio, television, etc.) that runs the advertisement charges a fee. Generally the more people you can reach, the more the advertisement costs. The term "costs per thousands" refers to the cost of the advertisement divided by the number of thousands of people who subscribe to the newspaper or magazine or who listen to the radio or watch the TV program. If you telemarket or do direct mail advertising, you have to pay the people who are making the telephone calls or pay for the printing and postage.

Research the costs of advertising in at least three different media. Find out not only how much an advertisement costs but also how many people each medium reaches.

medium 1	medium 2	medium 3
_____	_____	_____
cost	cost	cost
_____	_____	_____
number of people	number of people	number of people
_____	_____	_____

Choose one product to advertise. Considering the cost and reach of each medium, which medium would be best for your product and the target audience you hope to reach? Why?

product _____

medium _____

why _____

_____

Selling Your Product

Pretend that you are the head of an advertising agency. Not only do you create ads but you also advise your clients on which medium to use. You can choose from any or all of the media listed below. All of these will allow your clients to reach and influence a large number of people. Under what conditions (or for what reasons) would you advise them to choose each of these media?

television_____

_____

radio_____

_____

newspapers_____

_____

magazine _____

_____

Internet _____

_____

direct mail_____

_____

billboards _____

_____

Ad Time

Different media make most of their income by the fees they charge for advertising. While it sometimes seems like it would be nice if we didn't have to listen to, watch, or read so many advertisements, without the money these ads generated for the owners of these media, we would have to pay a lot more for our television service, our newspapers and our magazines.

Find out how much time or space is devoted to advertising in each medium. Analyze a half an hour of television, half an hour of radio, a newspaper and a magazine to find out what percentage of their time or space is devoted to advertisements. Combine your results with your classmates' findings on a graph.

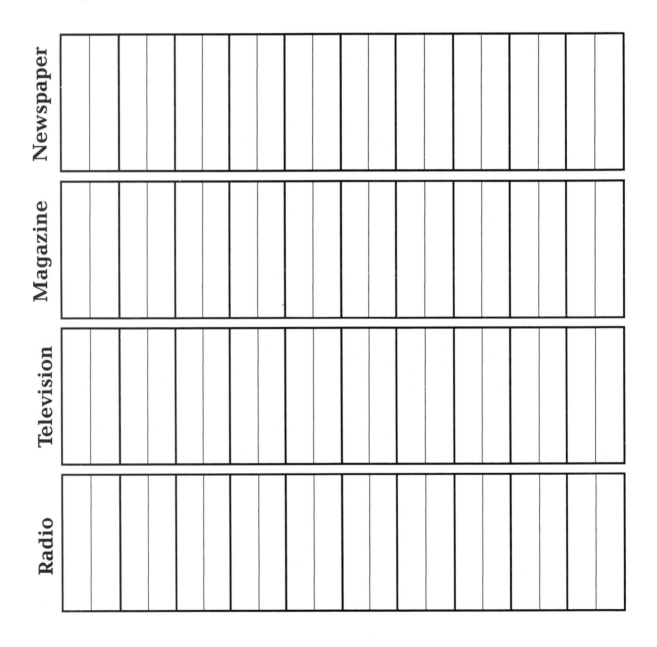

Radio Advertising

Radio has often been called the "theater of the mind." It is a medium that uses sound to stir the imagination and create images. Radio advertisements must create an image for people without showing any pictures. Some of the strategies that radio advertisers use are:

- **Selecting sensory words** - Words should create images in the minds of the listeners.

- **Avoid cliches** - Phrases that everyone has heard again and again will not catch anyone's attention.

- **Use voices that stand out** - Create a change from the newscasters that listeners are used to hearing.

- **Use contrasting music** - Select music that is different than what the listener usually hears on this station.

- **Avoid vague superlatives** - Words like "hottest," "simply the best," or "unbeatable bargains" are used too often.

- **Don't insult your audience** - Don't tell them things they already know.

Special Projects

1. Listen to the radio and choose two commercials, one that you think is effective and one that you think is not very good. Compare the two, telling what is good and what is bad about each one.

2. Write and record a radio advertisement that will sell people on an idea (like supporting a candidate, donating blood, wearing seat belts, or not using drugs).

Radio Script

Great Ads
124 Park Avenue
Anytown, Anyplace 19991

Job no.: 1223-345-854   Radio Department
Program: Date: 1/5/00
Client: Air Mexico   Time: 60 seconds
Product: Visit Mexico   Network: station KSBV

Singers:
1. Pack your bags
2. Get ready to fly
3. We're making Mexico
4. A wonderful buy

Announcer:
5. Air Mexico announces new, incredibly low fares to Mexico
6. We call it wonderful!
7. You'll save 50%
8. Yes, 50%!
9. On your round trip.
10. No advance purchase is necessary.
11. Leave any day except Friday or Saturday.
12. Stay for 14 days to 3 months.
13. No other airline lets you enjoy Mexico for less.

Singers:
14. We have that certain flair.
15. That's the difference.
16. Other airlines may get you there.
17. But only Air Mexico will pamper you all the way.
18. What could be easier?
19. What could be cheaper?
20. What could be more relaxing?

Announcer:
21. For complete details and reservations, call
22. your travel agent or Air Mexico.

More Ways to Sell

In addition to the advertising techniques that you have already studied, there are other methods used in advertising to persuade you to buy the products, services or ideas. While magazines, newspapers and radio use some of these techniques, only television makes use of all of them. They are:

- **pace** - fast or slow
- **scale** - making the product bigger or smaller than it actually is
- **voice over** - a person who is heard but not seen
- **tone** - hard hitting or soft sell
- **music** - sets the mood
- **repetition** - saying it again and again
- **omission** - all of the facts about the product are not told
- **association** - promising adventure, social attractiveness, or a product just like Grandma used to use (old-time or home-made quality)
- **logos** - symbols designed to represent the product simply and memorably
- **created spokesperson** - usually someone who is famous and respected, but it could be a fictional person or animal that people will associate with the product
- **jingle** - a short saying designed to stay in your mind so you won't forget the product

Special Projects

1. Find at least five advertisements that use some of these techniques. Identify the product, describe the technique used and discuss how you felt about the advertisement.

2. Choose an advertisement and rewrite it using one or more of these techniques.

Matching Advertising and Audiences

For each of the following types of television programs, describe the audience and tell what products or services might be advertised on the program.

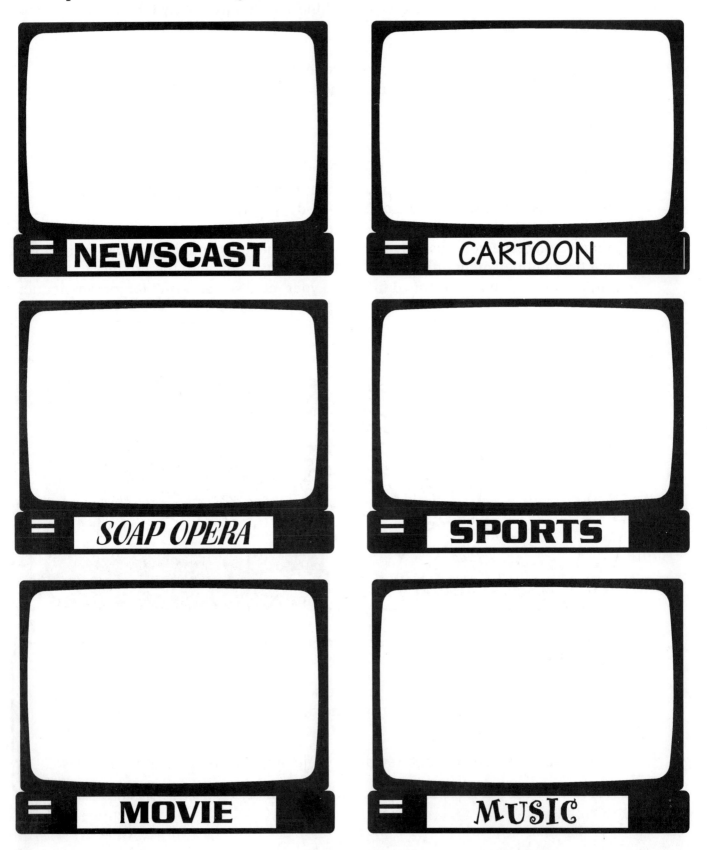

Television Advertising Survey

Use this chart to record the advertising techniques used for products sold on television. Write the names of the products and then record which advertising techniques are used. Also record the target audiences. Finally, record your rating of how persuasive the commercial was (+, ok, –).

Product	technique						target group					→rating
	weasel	image	name calling	plain folks	testimonial	bandwagon	children	parents	families	senior citizens	teenagers	
1.												
2.												
3.												
4.												
5.												
6.												
7.												
8.												
9.												
10.												

Your Own Television Commercial

Choose a product that you like. Create a storyboard for a commercial that uses one or more of the persuasion techniques.

❶

❷

❸

❹

❺

❻

Newspaper Advertising

Most of the money spent on advertising is for advertising in newspapers; however, this type of advertising is usually used by local businesses that are trying to reach people who live in the community. While there is some advertising in newspapers by national companies, generally if a company wants to reach consumers in a wider area, it would probably choose some other media. Advertisers typically will choose in which section of the newspaper they want their ads to run. For instance, if they are selling to mostly male, sports-minded customer's, they would choose the sports section.

Go through a newspaper (not the classified advertising section) and keep a record of the number of advertisements that are run for each kind of business. When you are finished tabulating the advertising space for each type of business, make a chart on another piece of paper to show the differences.

department stores	_____
grocery stores	_____
automobile	_____
furniture and household	_____
clothing	_____
financial	_____
amusements	_____
appliances, radio, television	_____
drugstore	_____
building supplies and services	_____
real estate	_____
hotels and restaurants	_____
jewelry	_____
other	_____

The Language of Advertising

Language has an influence over people and how they act. For this reason, advertisers choose their words carefully so that they convey the correct message and are effective in motivating people to act in a certain way. The visual appeal of an advertisement catches the viewer's eye and gets his attention, but the language that is used helps people understand and remember the product.

Advertisers usually use language that is positive and emphasizes the good qualities of what they are trying to sell. They may compare their product to another one or may just use superlatives (biggest, best, whitest, fastest, most honest) to tell how great their product is.

The fifteen most frequently used adjectives and verbs are:

adjectives	verbs
new	make
good/better/best	get
free	give
fresh	have
delicious	see
full	buy
sure	come
clean	go
wonderful	know
special	keep
crisp	look
fine	need
big	love
natural	use
real	feel

1. What kind of products would use the following words in their advertisements?

   fresh, delicious, and crisp _____

   fresh, clean, sure _____

   best, fine, real_____

2. On another piece of paper, write an advertisement for a product that uses at least three of the adjectives and two of the verbs from the list above.

Attention-Getters

A well-designed advertisement will grab the attention of people who see or hear it. For print ads this usually means that the advertisement includes:

A. headline - This is a large, easy-to-read, simply-stated, clever statement that gets your attention, It can be a single word or only a few words. It should convey one main idea or selling point. It has one function — to get the readers' attention. It should contain active, colorful words.

B. illustration - The illustration (drawing or photograph) should support the headline and demonstrate the claim that is made.

C. subhead - Some advertisements have a subheading that is in smaller type than the headline. It elaborates on the headline or introduces other features.

D. sales talk - The advertisement also has a section of information that is usually in much smaller type than the headline. It gives the reader more information, offers proof of any claims made in the headline and persuades him or her to take action (buy the product). This should be as convincing as possible.

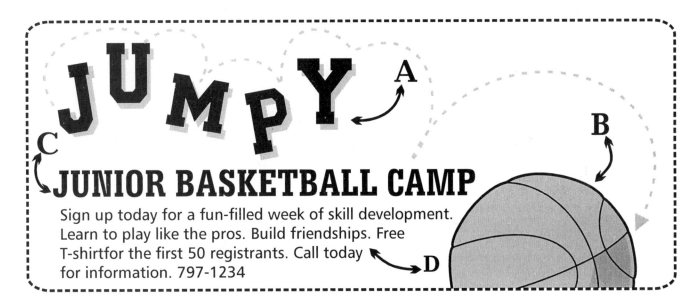

Special Projects

1. Select several printed advertisements and analyze how special layout techniques are used. Look for things like placement of headlines and pictures, use of bright colors, attractive pictures, and attention-getting words. Mount the advertisements along with your analysis of why the ads are effective.

2. Draw or cut out a picture of a product. Paste it in the middle of a piece of paper. Use this as the beginning of an advertisement. Include a headline, sales talk, appeal to a human need and an offer.

Analyzing Print Ads

Choose a printed advertisement and paste it on this page.
Identify each of the following things in the advertisement:
A. headline
B. illustration (or something to draw your attention)
C. sales talk (copy that explains the headline)
D. the offer (special price, discount, bonus)
E. the appeal (the human need)

Product Evaluation

Choose a product and test it to see if it lives up to the advertised claims.

Product name _____

Cost _____

Where purchased _____

Manufacturer _____

Quality tested for _____

Describe testing procedure_____

_____

_____

_____

_____

Test results _____

_____

_____

Does the product live up to the advertised claims? Explain_____

_____

_____

Your recommendations based on the results of this test _____

_____

_____

Advertising Watchdogs

There are several agencies that regulate advertising or suggest standards to make sure that advertisements are truthful. The intent of all of the agencies is to make sure that advertising is fair and that consumers will not be mislead into buying something that is not as good as the advertising claims it is. Advertisers may tell about all the good features of their products and why you should buy them, but they cannot say things that are deceptive. Some of the advertising watch dogs are:

- Council of Better Business Bureaus
- Federal Trade Commission
- American Association of Advertising Agencies
- American Advertising Federation
- Children's Advertising Review Unit

All of these organizations have some kind of guidelines for advertisements. The American Association of Advertising Agencies' code of conduct for its members prohibits advertising that includes:

- false or misleading statements
- testimonials that do not reflect the real choice of experts
- misleading price claims
- unsupported claims
- offensive statements, pictures or suggestions
- unfair comparisons

Special Projects

1. Write a list of three to five other standards or rules that you think should govern advertising.

2. Contact one of these organizations by mail or via the Internet. Get a copy of its code of ethics or regulations. Use this to evaluate four different advertisements.

Advertisement Comparison

Select two varieties of the same product (two different kinds of cereal, soap, gum, tennis shoes, drinks, etc.). Then answer the following questions about these two products.

The two products I compared are:

Product 1	Product 2
_____	_____

1. Find advertisements for the two products and identify the advertising techniques used.

Product 1	Product 2
_____	_____
_____	_____
_____	_____

2. At what target groups were the advertisements aimed?

Product 1	Product 2
_____	_____
_____	_____
_____	_____

3. What image was the advertiser trying to create (status, youth, excitement, etc.)?

Product 1	Product 2
_____	_____
_____	_____
_____	_____

4. How was this image achieved in the advertisement?

Product 1	Product 2
_____	_____
_____	_____
_____	_____

5. What are the strong selling points for each advertisement? For example, "this is good for you," "this product will change your life," "this will make things easier."

Product 1	Product 2
_____	_____
_____	_____
_____	_____

6. What kind of attention-getting words — words like "new," "improved," or "fantastic" — are used? Is the advertisement mostly fact or opinion?

Product 1	Product 2
_____	_____
_____	_____
_____	_____

7. How does the packaging of the product add to the sales appeal?

Product 1	Product 2
_____	_____
_____	_____
_____	_____

8. What are your criteria for a good advertisement?

_____

_____

9. Using these criteria, which advertisement did you find to be most appealing or persuasive? Why?

_____

_____

10. Which product would you choose? Why?

_____

_____

_____

11. What ideas do you have for improving the products or the advertisements?

Product 1	Product 2
_____	_____
_____	_____
_____	_____

Advertisement Survey

Choose three products in the same category. Cut out three print advertisements for the products or tape record three of the products' radio or television commercials. Survey your class members to find out what product they would purchase. Also find out if they were persuaded by the advertisements, the package designs, or some other factors.

Product category _____

Product 1	Product 2	Product 3
number choosing the product	number choosing the product	number choosing the product
persuaded by advertisement	persuaded by advertisement	persuaded by advertisement
package design	package design	package design
other	other	other

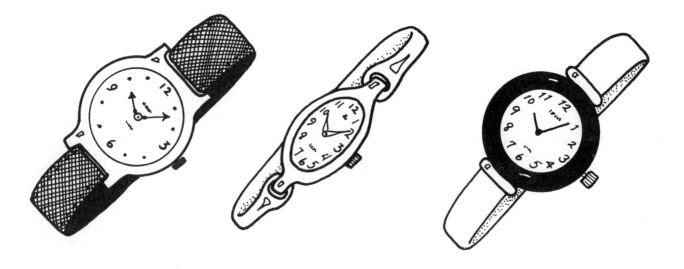

Debatable Topics

Advertising is an important ingredient of our free market economy. Without the ability of advertisers to take their messages to a large number of people, manufacturers would not be able to sell their products, political candidates would not be able to present their positions, and consumers would have a hard time finding out about new products or services. There are, however, many criticisms of advertising. Not everything about it is positive.

Form debate teams to debate one of the following issues. Have one side take the position as it is stated and the other side take the opposing position.

Resolved: Advertising directed toward children should be limited.

Resolved: Advertising of potentially harmful products like cigarettes and alcohol should be banned.

Resolved: Advertising has an unfavorable influence on television programming.

Resolved: Advertising is good for the economy.

Resolved: All programming for young children should be free of advertisements.

Resolved: You can't believe everything you hear or see in advertisements.

Resolved: Advertising is annoying and exaggerated.

Your Own Advertising Agency

Now that you know all about advertising, you're ready to start your own advertising agency. Choose one of the following types of products or services.

- a new soft drink
- a line of clothing for toddlers
- a local store selling flowers, gifts and cards
- a company specializing in creating web sites
- a house cleaning service
- a local Italian restaurant
- a national chain of fast-food restaurants
- a line of food and supplies for backpackers
- a dance studio
- a person running for city council

Plan an advertising campaign. You must present a plan that includes which media you will advertise in and at least one sample advertisement for each chosen medium. Start your ideas here and continue on another piece of paper. Your final presentation will be an **oral presentation** with accompanying **examples** (storyboard, ad layout, or radio script).

Wacky Product

Choose six products and change the names to
make humorous new products — for example,
Footsie Rolls or Gloom toothpaste. Then select one
of the products and create a wacky, yet convincing
advertisement, for this comical new product.

New Product Names

_____   _____   _____

_____   _____   _____

Advertisement
Start your ideas here for the print ad, the radio script or the television storyboard. Attach
the finished project.

Advertising and You

This is an opportunity for you to think about why you purchase some of the items you do and analyze what kind of advertising has an effect on your buying habits. Answer the following questions.

1. In general, how does advertising affect people's purchasing decisions?

_____

_____

_____

2. What techniques of advertising do you think are most convincing for people your age?

_____

_____

_____

3. Describe a recent time when your decision to buy something was a direct response to advertising.

_____

_____

_____

4. How will your knowledge of advertising techniques affect your future purchasing decisions?

_____

_____

_____

HURRY *before offer expires!*

Fantastic savings!

back to School **sale**

SUPER Selection